Pacharán Dreams

The Pamplona Poems

Marilyn Kiss

Plain View Press
P.O. 42255
Austin, TX 78704

plainviewpress.net
pk@plainviewpress.net
512-441-2452

Copyright © 2011 Marilyn Kiss. All rights reserved under International and Pan-American Copyright Conventions. No part of this book may be reproduced or distributed in any form or by any means, or stored in a data base or retrieval system, without written permission from the author. All rights, including electronic, are reserved by the author and publisher.

ISBN: 978-1-935514-97-8
Library of Congress Control Number: 2011917820

Cover art: Marilyn Kiss and miguelÁngel
Cover design by Pam Knight

Acknowledgements

"The Pamplona Alphabet," *Nimbus*, Wagner College, Staten Island, NY: Spring, 2009, (24-26). "The Song, The Song", *Nimbus*, Wagner College, Staten Island, NY: Spring, 2009, (44).

I would like to thank editor Susan Bright for reading this manuscript and accepting it for publication. Her death in December, 2010, left a pall over those who worked with her at Plain View Press and over any of us who met her through the years at AWP conferences. Her indomitable spirit stays with us still...as do memories of the convention parties and readings she organized for her authors. Thanks to Pam Knight for picking up where Susan left off...

Deepest appreciation to COAHSI. The publication of this book and subsequent readings are made possible in part by a DCA Premier Grant from the Council on the Arts & Humanities for Staten Island, with public funding from the New York City Department of Cultural Affairs.

I would like to thank *mi gente*, the many friends who have participated in the festival with me through the decades: Manolo, Ölle, Cristo, Alfonso, Antonio, Kathy and Leo, Nina, Takyo and Mari Paz, Rafa, Magda, Andrés, Pencho, Mikel, Andreas, José Miguel and many others who danced through the streets singing "Riau, Riau." The photographs show how much we enjoyed our time together in Pamplona! For Miguel, mis gracias y mucho amor. May we have many more *fiestas* together!

Particular appreciation to the people of Pamplona who open their hearts, their houses, and their city to international revelers and provide a yearly opportunity for truly *living in the moment*.

*To the existential spirit of the
Festival of San Fermín*

Contents: Pacharán Dreams

Preface   11

Anticipation   15

    Pacharán Dreams   17
    Ode to Pacharán   19
    The Pamplona Alphabet   22
    The Song, the Song   26
    "Uno de Enero…."   29
    2 de Febrero   30
    3 de Marzo   31
    4 de Abril   32
    5 de Mayo   33
    6 de Junio   34
    7 de Julio…¡San Fermín!   35
    En Route   36
    Don Ernesto   37
    Destination   38

Celebration   39

    El 6 de Julio   41
    El 7 de Julio   43
    El 8 de Julio   47
    The Running.   48
    El 9 de Julio   49
    El 10 de Julio   51
    Tercio de Banderillas   54
    El 11 de Julio   56
    El 12 de Julio   57
    El 13 de Julio   59
    El 14 de Julio   61

Separation 63

Pobre de Mí 65
Mi Gente 66
Plácido Domingo 74
Farewell, Pacharán 75
Pobre de Nosotros 77
El 15 de Julio 78
The Goring 81
If I Were a Bull... 83
It Feels Like Pamplona... 84
Sacrament 87
Pacharán Doubts 88
A Pamplona Poem 89

About the Author 93

Patxaran

From Wikipedia, the free encyclopedia

Patxaran (Basque pronunciation: [patʃaran]) (Basque from *baso aran* "wild plum", Spanish: *Pacharán*) is a sloe-flavoured liqueur commonly drunk in Navarre, the Pyrenees and elsewhere in Spain. It is usually served as a digestif either chilled or on ice.

Process

Patxaran is made by soaking sloe berries, collected from the blackthorn shrub, along with a few coffee beans and a vanilla pod in anisette. The process produces a light sweet reddish-brown liquid around 25-30% in alcohol content by volume. In addition to dictating the amount of sloe to be used, the regulating body for Pacharán Navarro insists that no colourings or flavourings be added and that the maceration last between one and eight months.

History

Known to have existed in Navarre as early as the Middle Ages, Patxaran was initially a home-made liqueur of rural Navarre and became popular during the late 19th century. It was commercialised in the 1950s and then became very popular outside Navarre. One theory for this rise holds that young Navarrese took bottles with them while on National Service, thereby popularising Patxaran throughout Spain. Currently, there are moves to ensure that the drink's name will be protected in order to ensure its quality, tradition and Navarrese identity.

A bottle of Zoco

Commercial brands and production

First sold in 1956, the oldest commercial brand is *Zoco*, founded by the family of Ambrosio Velasco, who had been producing patxaran in the Viana area since 1816. This brand is now owned by Pernod Ricard. Other brands include *Etxeko*, *Kantxa*, *Barañano Atxa* and *Baines*.

Preface

It was my first day in Spain, September 1968, when I met Manuel Varela at Cibeles in the center of Madrid. Of course I had read Ernest Hemingway's *The Sun Also Rises* as a high school student in Missouri and was planning to visit Pamplona and participate in the fiesta after my Master's degree year at Middlebury. His famous novel had popularized San Fermín for the English-speaking world. But it would be Manolo, who had been to Carnival in Río de Janeiro and many other world-class celebrations all over Europe and the Americas, who said I had to go to *los Sanfermines*, who said there was nothing like it, who said it was the greatest nine-day festival the world had to offer, who said that everyone participated, from newborns to nonagenarians.

He has managed unfailingly to go every year in the interim; I have been only 19 different summers...but it is just as he said it would be....the most incredible experience, the existential highlight of living both *in* and *for* the moment and having the sensation that the rest of the world has receded and the planet has continued to turn.

Manolo also introduced me to Pacharán....and the Technicolor dreams began.

Pacharán Dreams

The Running   Photo by miguelÁngel

Anticipation

Pacharán Dreams

Kodachromatic
technicolor
oftentimes three-dimensional
an Imax of the oeniric,
I worship you,
my pacharán dreams.

I seek you…
I search for you in the pacharán desert
of New York,
I troll for you
in the
political disaster of
Red States-Blue States,
I Google for you
in the pacharán wasteland
of cyberspace.

I seek the buzz around the edges
the onomatopoeia of
filled canvases,
of context
of desire
of lust
of blood

I want the night
to be a pacharán night,
I want the day
to be a pacharán day,
I want the experience
to be one fueled by pacharán,
I want existence to be
colored by the reddish glow
of pacharán.

Marilyn Kiss

I want the adrenaline always
of the
Running of the Bulls
in Pamplona.

Ode to Pacharán

If only all clothing were
the color of pacharán
silk especially or velvet for
all holidays
If only all cars were
the color of pacharán
the highway a canvas
the roadway an inebriating swirl,
a museum of the senses in perpetual motion.

If only all houses were
the color of pacharán
Suburbs of pigments,
skyscrapers of pixels
reflecting the joy of the
refracted rays on a bottle of Zoco.

If only we could view the world
through pacharán tinted glasses.

The tincture of pacharán would
color our souls, form us into
an infinite parade
marching towards Pamplona.

If only all of our dreams could
be pacharán dreams
If only all of our nightmares could
be exorcised by pacharán.

Pacharán, sometimes you elicit memories
of the Running
from my pacharán youth,
my pacharán prime.

Marilyn Kiss

Sometimes, infrequently, they are lachrymose
More often jubilant
as the Basque euphoria invades
my bones.

Often, often, oh pacharán,
but not often enough,
son of anisette and endrina berries,
You Rule my World.
I have pacharán friends,
pacharán lovers,
a cadre who knows the special drunkenness
of an empty glass, an empty bottle.

In fall, I dream of the magic elixir
In winter, I think of the nascent flavor
In spring, I consider the emerging berry
In summer, I reap the harvest
on the 7th of July.

If I were in Neruda's desert
I would long for your liquid succor
as la Bella Durmiente languished for the kiss.

My love, my pacharán flavored love,
you must be one with me
during the Running of the Bulls in Pamplona
You must devote your summer days
to mythic pursuits of Minoan proportions.

You must come with me
and be my all,
the pacharán of my days
that nourishes my cells, the fiber of my being,
a member of the circle
of pacharán inebriated acolytes.

Pacharán Dreams

May everyone drink from
the bottle of pacharán
that he or she may remember
in each tinted drop
the celebratory days,
the ecstatic nights,
the festival of San Fermín,
the Running of the Bulls
in Pamplona.

Marilyn Kiss
The Pamplona Alphabet

Always, always on the streets of
Pamplona, the triple "a's" of pacharán.

Bibulous hordes discover the Basque liqueur.

Countless novices from the global Diasporas
order the drink
on the Plaza del Castillo.

Devotees seek refuge
in technicolor pacharán dreams.

Ernest Hemingway sits in stony guard,
honored at the entrance
to the Plaza de Toros.

Existential Pamplona.
Exhilarating and *siempre*
exemplary.

May the Estafeta be the final
resting place
of my ashes.

¡Fiesta! ¡Fiesta! ¡Fiesta!
For whom does the bell toll?

Gigantes representing continents
swirl dizzily through the blurry mornings,
dance rhythmically through the heavy afternoons.

How does one live without Pamplona?

Homage due to Don Ernesto,
popularizer of the *fiesta*,
even though it flourished
prior to his rising sun.

Pacharán Dreams

I exist in Pamplona
I emerge in Pamplona
I embody the international spirit
of Pamplona.

Jake has nothing on me for
I, too, traverse the
drunken landscape of 3:00 a.m.
as Calle Jarauta shifts beneath my feet.

Kindness ebbs and flows.
Kilos of bovine flesh run, fight, lunge,
charge, suffer, expire, nourish.
Kids from all over the planet
come for the ecstasy of the Running.

Love Pamplona
Live Pamplona
Leave Pamplona

Morir thinking of Pamplona
because it was where
you felt most alive.

Never relinquish
the pacharán dreams
of Pamplona…
Nunca….Jamás.

Open your senses
to the phantasmagorical splendor
of Pamplona.
Open your nights
to the oneiric aftermath of the festival.

Open yourself to living in the moment.

Marilyn Kiss

Pamplona,
Plaza de Toros,
Pacharán,
Plamplona,
Plaza del Castillo,
País Vasco
Planeta.

*¿Quién puede negar, quién puede evitar
la llamada de Pamplona?
¿La seducción de Pamplona?*

¿Otro vaso de pacharán?

*Riau, Riau,
Riau, Riau…*

In the name of
San Fermín,
a sensorial stew
swirling, swaying,
sifting, stumbling,
singing, swinging
stirring
along the Calle San Nicolás,
the semiotics of the Festival.

The TOROS
grazing in the pastures,
running through the streets,
fighting in the bullring,
The mythical, symbolical, all too *carne y hueso*
 toros of Pamplona.

Today!
Today!
Today!
Tomorrow does not exist.
Yesterday never was.
It's the moment
and the ---ing form of the verb.

Ubiquitous euphoria
of existence.

Verifiable, palpable,
¡Viva San Fermín! ¡Gora!

Wanton nights
evolving into
a *Weltanschauung* of celebration.

Oompah bands blaring
to xylophone accompaniment

the yin and yang of existence,
the yearlong yearning
for the 7th of July.

Hands reach out for another glass of Zoco.

Marilyn Kiss

The Song, the Song

Aural,
acoustic,
unrhymed

The song,
the song,
permeates the skin,
invades the membranes,
ushers its fantasies
into the nuclei of the cells.

The song,
the song,
is in the heart,
is on the calendar,
is the essence of the spin
around the sun.

The song,
the song,
reels its way
through the snows
of January
uno de enero
the drifts of February
dos de febrero
the slushes of March
tres de marzo
the buds of April
cuatro abril
the blossoms of May
cinco de mayo
the fruitions of June.
seis de junio

Pacharán Dreams

The song,
the song,
leads us
through the calendar
through the centuries,
through the *calles*
of Pamplona.

We harken to its call.

We stand at attention
to its harmonies.

We listen.

We buy our tickets.
We make our reservations.
We heed the summons.

We arrive, on schedule,
for the
Running of the Bulls
in Pamplona.

siete de julio
¡San Fermín!

Marilyn Kiss

La Bota   Photo by miguelÁngel

"Uno de Enero...."

December days darken, shorten,
then switch gears.
Festivities mask the underlying memory,
the surge in the synapses,
the quickening in the veins.

The calendar runs on empty.
The year labors to its end.

The song explodes in its anticipation,
its newness, its repetition
its desires for the sun to return to
the House of the Crab.

From beneath the snow, the ice,
in subfreezing temperatures,
it explodes in the mouth,
it resounds in the ear
it lives in the DNA
of acolytes awaiting
the call to journey to
Pamplona.

It flounders, seeking volume.
It shudders, seeking a chorus.
It stutters, seeking warmth, energy,
a recharging.

It arises, as surely as revelers
on the opening day of a virgin year,
echoing across the highways and byways

"Uno de enero............San Fermín."

We put ourselves in neutral as the wait begins.

Marilyn Kiss
2 de Febrero

The hunger moon waxes and wanes.

Blood sluggish.
Appetites on hold,
the initiated sing
the second verse.

Lunar phases pass inexorably.

The cold enters
through the eyes,
freeze-dries the lungs,
settles in the soul.

A knighted rodent emerges,
predicts and scurries,
finds glaring winter sun and shadow…
or not.

Dense icy skies. Nothing changes.

Longing for the vernal equinox,
for signs of renewal,
waiting for the song
to carry us onward, closer
to Pamplona.

Dos de febrero….
San Fermín.

3 de Marzo

The surge is in the cells,
an awakening of sorts,
a false glimmer of the aperture to come.

It will be sung, the song,
among those who construct their year,
who guide their lives, divide their days
around Pamplona.

It will be shared
among the minions
who await with pleasant anxiety
the approaching chaos.

The calendar always slow…
Fast the years, then the decades…
but slow the approaching
of each marking,
each hallowed march
towards Pamplona.

Tres de marzo…
San Fermín.

Marilyn Kiss
4 de Abril

What does T.S. Eliot
have to do with it?

April is the cruelest month
with or without him,

the halfway point
between the new year
and the year
as acolytes know it.

The authentic annual peregrination
to Pamplona,
closer,
but still so distant

The fiesta

The bulls

The pacharán

We need celestial confirmation
We need terrestrial grounding

We need, we need

We need T. S. Eliot.
We need April.

Cuatro de abril…
San Fermín

5 de Mayo

Cinco de mayo is not just Mexican,
not just margaritaville,
not just tequila and tacos.

Cinco de mayo is a station
of the cross
on the road
to the sacred hills of Pamplona.

Cinco de mayo means stellar configurations
in clear skies,
means air that caresses the skin,
means oxygen against flesh.

Cinco de mayo
heightens
the desire
for a pacharán
in Pamplona.

Cinco de mayo
means we are all
closer to ecstasy.

Cinco de mayo…
San Fermín.

Marilyn Kiss
6 de Junio

The nearness overwhelms.

It is palpable,
the plaza brimming with life,
the streets alive with dancing,
the bullring dancing with death,
the bars exhaling the essence of Pamplona.

The synapses coalesce
around the countdown
to the festival.

Anís and endrina berries steep their magic.

The air holds promises,
secrets,
dreams.

The city is on the verge of eruption.
The people are ready for the explosion,
 the *chupinazo*.

But it is June.

Everything is on hold.
The waiting continues....

Seis de junio...
San Fermín.

7 de Julio...¡San Fermín!

The fiesta explodes
as Hemingway said it would,
and we are but spectators, minor players,
for it is the bulls, the bulls, who run and lunge and fight
and die.

Colors...phantasmagorical.

Sounds...musical, multinational, multilingual.

Tastes rooted in the Basque cuisine.

Smells reel through the air
beyond the capacity
of human appreciation.

Tactile sensations include
the trajectory of a *buñuelo de crema*
in its trip
across the tongue.

Longing for Pamplona is a calling.

Living for Pamplona requires a résumé.

Loving Pamplona demands devotion to
experiencing the moment to its fullest.

Siete de julio...
San Fermín.

Marilyn Kiss
En Route

Throbbing our way to Pamplona,
cultural lemmings, migratory wildebeests,
swirling monarchs
winging towards the Basque heartland
the existential home in our hearts.

Songs lifted en masse
drumming on a seat, a table,
a suitcase
Shouting for glee at the
cyclical nature of life
at the rotation of the planet on its axis
at the turning again into
the celebratory season

Discovering each other in the great migration
a common destiny

No introduction; none needed
the crimson bandanna, the blazing sash
the song, yes the omnipresent song

"Uno de enero, dos de febrero…
siete de julio
¡SAN FERMIN!"

Pacharán Dreams

Don Ernesto

Your statue huddles
as stalwart guardian
of the entrance
to the bullring,
greets international pilgrims
with its stony stare

An obligation met
as revelers pay homage,
as they recall
your role in the multinational
metamorphosis of Pamplona
in July

Popularizer of the festival
Promoter of its revelry
Prose celebrant of its
exuberance

FIESTA

*"The things that happened
could only have happened
during a fiesta. Everything
became quite unreal finally
and it seemed as though
nothing could have any
consequences. It seemed out
of place to think
of consequences
during the fiesta."*
The Sun Also Rises

Would Jake and Lady Brett
spend their time texting,
search for themselves on YouTube,
post to Facebook?

Marilyn Kiss
Destination

Beyond, beyond, always farther beyond.

If one pacharán is a foothold in this
deeply sought realm,
it's the second glass that
proffers entrance,
the third a seat at the table.

But what if one desires residence,
a legitimacy in a land
where the mundane recedes,
visions explode,
imaginary colors reign,
cosmic connectedness seems possible,
and life, for a moment, becomes bearable?

What transports,
transgresses,
transcends?

It's not guaranteed, assured, even justifiable.
Nine days in Pamplona
provide the sacred portal.

Altered states, alternate reality,
beyond the quotidian.

Celebration

Marilyn Kiss

Chupinazo   Photo by miguelÁngel

El 6 de Julio

Pilgrims arriving, continuing to arrive,
drawn by the song thrumming in the blood
following paths worn by centuries of use

Crowds amassing, greeting,
shouting, shifting, stamping
carousing, w a i t i n g
The excitement palpable
hanging over us
like the breath
of a heated beast

Destination: the *Ayuntamiento*
garbed in medieval glory
stolid stone structures standing
in contrast to the human swarm,
buzzing below
arms raised, chanting the song, the song

Frenetic moments, movements
the blood swirling to an annual rhythm
released from hibernation.

The crescendo of the wait
The excitement mounting
escalating,
pulsating, pulsating
into that collective
champagne-soaked
rocket-signaled
much heralded
orgasm,
the *chupinazo*.

As Don Ernesto wrote,
"the fiesta exploded."

Marilyn Kiss

El Encierro

Photo by
miguelÁngel

El 7 de Julio

El encierro.
The first,
the heart,
the core,
the marrow of
the festival.

"Uno de enero….
siete de julio…"

SAN FERMIN.

Energy increasing,
Anticipation.
Waiting.
Anticipation.
Sweating.
Anticipation mounting.
Anticipation
Anticipation
Anticipation.

3:00 a.m.
Still time to pass the *bota*
Still time to order another *pacharán*
Still time to dance another *jota*
in the Plaza del Castillo.

4:00 a.m.
Dark though
there's
a brightening in the
eastern sky.

Marilyn Kiss

Must move,
must jostle and dance,
must lemming
our way
to the barricades,
barter positions,
trade spaces,
seek a privileged view.

5:00 a.m.
Tension,
electric,
a current of runners and
revelers
crowding the streets.
A shock wave.

6:00 a.m.
Light spreads.
Buildings emerge
from the medieval shadows.
Stores appear
in their plywood
protections
along the Estafeta.
Streets smell
freshly washed,
reinvigorated, renewed.

Garbage accumulates.
Altercations arise.
Tempers flare.

All in good fun,
all in the spirit of the Festival.

Shoving increases
as multitudes
await
the celebrated
Running.

7:00 a.m.
Runners gather
in drunken revelry.
Revelers gather
in drunken anticipation.
Viewers appear
at windows, balconies,
overlooking the Cuesta de Santo Domingo,
the Ayuntamiento,
the Mercaderes,
the Curva leading into the Estafeta,
the Telefónica,
the dead-end street to the bullring.

The fabled cobblestones
of history and literature
of cruelty and culture
of early mornings in Pamplona
in July.

"San Fermín bendito…"
rings inebriated
from the mouths of the runners,
a supplication,
an entreaty,
a plea for safety for femurs and fibulas
in front of the
horns and heart
of the mythical, carnal,
BULL.

"….Bendición."

Marilyn Kiss

8:00 a.m.
and the rockets
the explosion
the mass of runners
pressing as ONE
the collective body
the moment
the movement
the masses
the madness.

Two minutes
of panic and pandemonium

Of the press of crowds,
of the hordes
of fun
of horns
of bulls
Running
through the fabled streets
during the
first *encierro* of the
Festival.

Spectators on edge.
The primodial forces released
The encounter of
man and beast
along the legendary route
of the
Encierro in Pamplona.
Day 2.

El 8 de Julio

Día tres.

The second morning of the Running.

Stories to share
Experiences to narrate.
Anecdotes.
Anecdotes.
Anecdotes.

Over *café*.
Over *café con leche*.
Over a *carajillo*.
Over *anís*.
Over *pacharán*.

Day One is documented
in amplified photos
over the Plaza del Castillo.

Not to worry.
There are still
seven spaces for updated images.

The Festival is in progress.
It provides repetition, release,
recurrence, RESACA,
remembrances, reunions,
repetition, release.

Sleep is absent still,
stalking.
Sleep dwells in the shadows
waiting to pounce, feline,
into the bovine spectacle.
Sleep seems so realistic,
so other-worldly,
so non-Pamplona.

Marilyn Kiss

The Running

The Running.
Two minutes fifty-eight seconds.

A goring.
The femoral artery.
Emergency.
Preparedness.
Pamplona
on alert.

Embraces,
encounters,
enchantments, numerous.

Casa Paco,
"huevos con patatas"
(Somos vegetarianos....
¡en Pamplona!).

The swing, the sway,
the sway and swagger
the swagger and the stumble…

It's the third day
in Pamplona.

Bullfight tickets.
Cruelty incarnate.
Festival encapsulated, conscience questioned.

PARADOX.

Loving it, living it,
dreading it, spreading it,
Pamplona…

Day Three.

El 9 de Julio

Accumulation.

Alcohol in the blood.
Pacharán in the dreams.
Memories in the cerebral cortex.

Bulls and humans
locked in a savage minuet.

It is the third day
of the Running.

Crowds mingle and swarm,
musicians meet and participate,
runners drink and petition.

"San Fermin, bendito…"
in spite of previous betrayals.
"San Fermín, bendito…"
in spite of rampant consumerism.

"San Fermín, bendito…"
in spite of there being no oxygen left
on the streets of Pamplona.

"San Fermín bendito…"
because your space belongs
to us.

We are your acolytes.
We serve you.
We run in your honor,
through the streets of
Pamplona,
during the FIESTA.

Marilyn Kiss

In other months,
we bare our teeth,
display our horns.

Pacharán Dreams

El 10 de Julio

Fiesta in full swing,
diurnal, nocturnal rhythms
following ancient patterns.

Morning crowds mill and mingle,
chocolate and *churros,*
coffee and rolls,
dreary-eyed or
fresh-faced
depending on
degree of decadence,
of debauchery.

Children are scrubbed and awaiting
the parade of the giants.
Through the streets
they will sashay from plaza to plaza
swirling and swaying
eight magnificent doll-statues
on stilts.
Male and female, they are,
representing the continents,
answering the human need
for rites and rituals,
for a *fiesta*.

The big-headed *cabezudos*
will chase the young crowd
in their bright white shirts,
their ironed red kerchiefs,
chasing and hitting the incautious
taunting and running,
feather weapons ready for
the mischievous grin,
the audacious smirk.

Marilyn Kiss

It's time for
the midday feasts,
friends reunited or recently made,
in restaurants, on street corners,
the *pisto* and the bulls,
the *caldo*, the omnipresent wine.

The ooompa-bands take over.
The local *peñas*
will control the afternoon,
leading revelers to the bullring.

The clock turns inexorably
to Lorca's hour.
"*A las cinco en punto de la tarde.*"
It will be 5:00 p.m. in the seats in the shade,
5:00 p.m. in the sun-drenched bleachers.

This fragment of time belongs to the bulls,
500 kilos of taut flesh.

It's their moment
to bleed in the sun,
to expire in the sand,
face cruelty beyond reason or measure.

Crowds drunk on adrenaline
and blood lust
await the ancient duel
between man and beast.

It's time for the bulls,
for greeting Hemingway
at the entrance to the *Plaza de Toros*.

It's the moment of truth.

Fanfare! Pomp and circumstance.
The entourage circles
the ring.

Tercio de varas

The handlers mount
their padded horses,
the picadors stab,
the first blood flows.

Marilyn Kiss

Tercio de Banderillas

The *banderilleros* twirl their *capotes*,
magenta and yellow
in the lengthening shadows.
Bugles blare,
the drunken crowd roars.
There is more blood.

Tercio de muerte

The matador's finest hour,
his suit of lights sparkling
his red *muleta* draped,
his sword positioned,
fear dulled,
his practiced hand
ready for the encounter.

The mortal ballet begins.

It's life or death.
It's essential.
It's eternal.

It's in the genes.

The aorta bursts
in a corolla of glory.

Indultos are rare,
steaks abundant.

It is 9:00 p.m.
in the Plaza de Toros
in Pamplona.

Day five of the fiesta.

Pacharán Dreams

Sidra   Photo by miguelÁngel

Marilyn Kiss
El 11 de Julio

The sun rises
languorously
on another
day in Pamplona.

Jake is not there.

Lady Brett Ashley
is already at the bar.

Don Ernesto sits
in stone silence
at the entrance to the bullring.

The sun will never
set on Pamplona.

Pacharán will keep Apollo
hopping into his chariot,
keep the crowds coming,
keep the fiesta flowing
along the streets of Navarre.

Day Six,
The Running of the Bulls.

El 12 de Julio

You are so absurd,
you unknown saint
named Fermín.

Even your title
smells like a bullpen.

Bleed in the streets
like those
who die
for your madness.

Vomit in the park
like the tourists
who come to worship
in your bodegas.

Shit behind the Plaza de Toros
because you just can't stomach
one more wine,
one more bull,
one more insult.

You and Hemingway
must be laughing
at this moment
as we engage in this ritual
with nervous tension
and profound disbelief.

Shake your macho fist in my face.

I will eat your festival
I will cross oceans to attend
I will dread and curse and suffer
I will long and yearn and remember

Marilyn Kiss

And I will be there in July.

Day Seven, San Fermín.

Pacharán Dreams

El 13 de Julio

It cannot be!

New friends still unmet,
pacharán still uncorked,
bulls still corralled,
waiting to run, to fight.

It cannot be!

In this timeless space,
this existential moment,
time does pass
according to clocks, calendars.

The festival heightens its intensity.
The beat quickens.
The movements are more frenetic.

The ebb and flow,
movement in circular time.

We will bite our own tail.
We will write our own tale.

So much still to experience!
So much still to recall!
So much, so much!

Overload of the eighth day.
No time, no time.

The festival cannot come to an end!
It must continue…
And it does.

Day eight…and counting.
Otro pacharán, por favor.

¡*Gora San Fermín!*

Marilyn Kiss

Waiting: *El encierro*   Photo by miguelÁngel

El 14 de Julio

We will cry tonight
but tonight does not yet exist.

We will light candles tonight
but this morning the bulls run,
the crowds cheer,
the runners dodge and dance
down the Estafeta.

It has rained.

Streets are dangerous
for runners and bulls.
Streets are crowded,
even more so
since this is the last *encierro*,
the last official morning
of the fiesta.

We hold onto it
since it must last a year.

We hold onto it
since it gives us sustenance.

We hold onto it
because, like for the bull,
it means life or death.

We hold on and keep on holding.

We perform the rituals of the day…
chocolate and churros
gigantes and cabezudos,
restaurant meals and oompah bands,
peñas and bullfights,
but it is *Pobre de mí* all day.

There is a melancholy in the moment.
There is a symbol of life.
There is our own existence encapsulated
in a day.

We are Pamplona.
Our blood is pacharán.

We strike a compromise
with time.

We drink a toast…
and yet another
to pacharán dreams.

Day Nine,
The Running of the Bulls
in Pamplona.

The Basque Country, Spain.

Separation

Marilyn Kiss

Pobre de Mí... Photo by miguelÁngel

Pobre de Mí

Pobre de mí, pobre de ti
Se nos acaban las fiestas de San Fermín

Surviving another year without Pamplona?

The wait
The anticipation
The adrenaline pumping through the blood
the existential ---ing on hold.

Candles, constellations of *velas*
aspirations, millions of them,
flickering in the Basque night.

We exhale,
We inhale,
We try to breathe
thinking of the 357 days
that separate us from
the next Pamplona.

Waltzing through the *callejuelas*
marching down the boulevards,
holding our lighted offerings on high,
kneeling, jumping,
singing, prancing…
our collective *velorio*

we pretend that
Pamplona is forever,
That the moment is
eternal.

Pobre de mí, pobre de ti

Jean Paul and Simone were right.

Marilyn Kiss
Mi Gente

> *Mi gente. ¡Ustedes!*
> *lo más grande de este mundo…*
> *yo los invitaré a gozar,*
> *conmigo sí van a gozar*
> *yo lo invitaré a gozar conmigo sí…*
> —Hector Lavoe

1.
Miguel

Always and forever
from el *"uno de enero"*
to *el 31 de diciembre*,
from the first *"Riau-riau"*
from *chupinazo* to *chupinazo*,
from *encierro* to *encierro*,
from bar to bar
from plaza to plaza
from decade to decade

to the final
"pobre de mí"

Share with me, my love
the pacharán dreams
the frenetic festival.

2.
Takyo:
The Blue Plastic Camera

Kneeling
squatting
circling
bending
Clicking,
imitating the Nikoners
as they attempted
to document
the phatasmagorical wonder
that is Pamplona

A reflection that would
meld into a single
entity,
a multifaceted friendship.

Photographer photographing and
photographed on film both
celluloid and Zen.

Thus it began…

The drinks shared
the festival experienced
the connections prolonged
the lives becoming complicated
and intertwined.

As circles widened
to encompass
latitudes and longitudes
beyond el País Vasco

Marilyn Kiss

As experiences broadened
to include
both sides of the Atlantic

as ties became stronger,

as moments became days,

days became months,

months became years,

years became decades,

As love threw its mantle over
this chance encounter,

as this existential moment
of the blue plastic camera
in the Plaza del Castillo
Pamplona, País Vasco,
Spain

became the compass,
the North Star,
a navigational center
of several
lives.

3.
Nina

Nina
barefoot or shod
Nina in the Plaza del Castillo
at lunch in the Otano
in the bars
of Calle Jarauta

Nina
alone or accompanied
with a gliding walk
and an air of contemplation
Nina in the bullring
or in the residence of la Señora
on San Nicolás

Nina in the sunshine
and in dappled shade
in stark daylight and
at dusk
in fiesta mode at dawn

Nina
watching the bulls
as they charge through
the streets of Pamplona

Nina
Brave, beautiful
with a *copa* of Pacharán

Nina
Always Nina
No memory of Pamplona
is complete without her
no Estafeta is imaginable,
no *encierro* is possible.

4.
Manolo

A stalwart central presence in Pamplona,
issuing the clarion call across the continents
to revelers speaking many languages,
you,
Manolo
of four decades of perfect attendance,
of four decades of friendships built and managed,

you,
you are integral.

Your voice touted the running
Your voice in Portuguese or Galician or French
Your voice in German or Spanish or impeccable English

Your voice saying, always repeating,
"There is nothing like it!
Nothing!
Gora San Fermín!"

5.
Ölle

Lumbering along
the Calle Jarauta
a Paul Bunyon in stained whites and reds

A giant Swede with
Pantagruelian appetites
for kilo fillets
pitchers of Black and tan
a night's worth of Pacharán.
kalimochos to greet the dawn

Always a John Lennon song
on his breath
always a Springsteen lyric to mutter
always "Gora San Fermín"
always praise for the "Vascus People."

A personage
A figurehead
A part of Pamplona for
more than four decades.

A call as the
New Year's countdown begins
"Uno de enero"
A post-fiesta message from
a balcony
in San Sebastián.

A Basque play should be named for Ölle.

I proclaim the "Ölleazo."

6.
Mikel

Bobbing, bouncing,
bursting with energy
superblonde
above the hordes
of mere mortals
A runner
facing the bulls
in the streets of Pamplona.

Sun-drenched fear now
to be able to resist
the long months of the
northern Swedish night.

A mythical beast
An ancient confrontation:
Real blood.

"San Fermín, bendito."

Newspaper rolled
alpargatas laced
kalimochos downed

Wound tight,
our Mikel,
seeking release in
the Basque summer,
solace in the Pacharán dreams
that will sustain him
through the Scandinavian winter.

7.
Rafa

Scowling
Rafa of the
deeply-furrowed
brow

The monk among us
with non-catholic proclivities

A loner of long mountain hikes,
early morning archery ranges,
and bone-crunching bike rides
through formidable
passes in los
Picos de Europa

Rafa
who prefers canine companionship
who opens his Pamplona *piso*
with generosity

Rafa
of ancient longings
and deep friendships
who seeks solitude
in July.

Marilyn Kiss
Plácido Domingo

Plácido Domingo,
neither placid
nor of Sunday school persuasions.

Plácido,
tenuous tenor
belting forth from the
southwest corner of the
Plaza del Castillo.

Plácido Domingo,
regaler of revelers
through the 80's and 90's
with vocal vibrations
reaching epic proportions.

A modern Don Quijote,
with invented garb,
your golden helmet,
a container for *aceitunas*,
your vestments reclaimed from the *basura*,
a lance from the realm
of the imagination.

Plácido,
caricature, characterized,
pulverized by the windmills
of the years.

Plácido,
sing for me in the insomniac nights
of my
pacharán dreams.

Farewell, Pacharán

Pacharán farewells
are lachrymose.

Pacharán farewells
leave an emptiness
in the body,
a deadness in the spirit,
a hole in the fabric of existence.

Pacharán farewells
are a nightmare.

Pacharán farewells
mean another year
without the infusion
of friendships nurtured,
rituals renewed,
bulls outrun,
photos taken,
drunken conversations
begun and forgotten.

If one must say farewell,
one needs pacharán.

Restaurante Photo by miguelÁngel

Pobre de Nosotros
Pobre de mí
pobre de ti
Pobre de all of us
who seek the
existential
living in the moment
that is Pamplona.

Pobre de the peasant from
the interior of Asturias
spending his Euros at the
carnival
Pobre de the gypsy
telling fortunes on the Plaza
Pobre de the African
selling trinkets on the streets
Pobre de the squatters
seeking refuge from the night
Pobre de the poor
struggling to survive.

Pobre de
Pobre de
Pobre de

Why is there so much poverty
in the prosperous nations?

Why does San Fermín not
intervene?

Pobre de mí
Pobre planeta

Pobre
Pobre
Pobre

Marilyn Kiss
El 15 de Julio

Sun sparkles
on the washed and swept
Plaza

Chairs neatly aligned
Tables in geometric procession
A meticulous Escher-like quality
pervades

Order
Decorum
Harmony
Normalcy

Where now the hordes,
the drunken
thousands?

Where now the
strolling families
dressed in white
and always, always
a red kerchief?

Where now the mayhem
and madness
of the world descending
on this northern Basque
city for a week outside
of time?

Nine days
Beyond calendar and chronometer

A backpacker
with bloodshot eyes
downs coffee and
croissant

Pacharán Dreams

A band of tourists
bumps suitcases
along the
thoroughfares

A couple
purchases mementoes
before hailing
a cab

There are no bulls

Was it all
just a
pacharán dream?

Marilyn Kiss

Aficionados Photo by miguelÁngel

The Goring

Cobblestones dew-dampened

Runners alcohol-fueled

Toros adrenaline-engorged…

A recipe for junction and collision
between beast and technological behemoth
on the curves of the Telefónica

Dawn the color of blood
over the *Cuesta de Santo Domingo*

Sky the density of *sangre*
above the *Plaza del Ayuntamiento*

Atmosphere charged
with the scent of blood
along the Estafeta

CONTACT.

The keratinized sheath
of bony core
meets the muscles and tendons
of the *gluteus maximus*
in a ritual as ancient as Minoan Crete

arteries and veins exposed, flesh rendered,

creating a moment of revenge

producing an instant of payback

for centuries of domestication and domination
for inhumane abattoirs and cruel *mataderos*,
for the yoke, the plow and the hamburger

Marilyn Kiss

Between runner or matador and bull,
equality is re-established ephemerally
in the evolutionary
scheme of things

In that terrible instant
when the soul illuminates
and surrenders
to the thousand-pound dark weight
of the knowledge
of human cruelty
to the bovine legacy,

when we admire and respect
if even for a moment,
the power and transcendence
of the mythological, symbolical,
raging and goring
Bull…

a bull, one of six, one of many,
in the streets and bullring
of Pamplona…

we accept primordial rules,
we submit to the majestic,
we intuit the divine.

Run, baby, run…

If I Were a Bull...

If I were a bull...

Beneath the black sun
Beneath the countless eyes
Beneath the bloody hour

Is that where I would choose
to end my days?

In the arena of deaf sounds
tempting the cape
surrounded by cheers and sunlight?

If I were a bull…

Above the passing instant
Above the white clamor
Above the footprints of death

Strident silence
heart pounding
awaiting the toreador's
sequined urgency

If I were a bull…

If I were a bull,
in Pamplona?

Marilyn Kiss
It Feels Like Pamplona…

Pulling an all nighter,
eyelids heavy, energy draining,
senses on edge,
synapses firing,
coffee perking, imagination soaring
feels like Pamplona.

Savoring the freshness of
a street-washed dawn,
breakfasting on *chocolate* and *churros*
in the middle of a thoroughfare
surrounded by ecstatic runners
returning from the Plaza
IS Pamplona.

Imbibing pacharán
in a glass pilfered
from Bar Txoco,
even when the pacharán is
from Galito's in Newark
feels like Pamplona.

Ordering pacharán *sin hielo*
in bars on the Jarauta
as international revelers
swirl and sway,
awaiting the *encierro*
IS Pamplona.

Dealing with a *resaca*,
mouth full of cotton,
tongue coated, vision blurred,
head in a vice being hit by
sledgehammers
feels like Pamplona.

Pacharán Dreams

Dealing with a *resaca*,
mouth full of cotton,
tongue coated, vision blurred,
head in a vice being hit by
sledgehammers
IS Pamplona.

Delirium, drunkenness,
euphoria, joy, altered states
always feel like Pamplona
as they evoke
an atemporality
that paradoxically exists
only between July 7 – July 15
on the streets,
in the plazas,
in the residences,
in the bars, restaurants, cafes,
of Pamplona,
the Basque Region,
Spain,
Europe,
Planet Earth,
Milky Way,
the Multiverse.

Doing the
"barefoot boogie on
the edge of the blade"
feels like Pamplona
whether in Manhattan or Manitoba,
whether in Chatanooga or Chicago,
whether in Seattle or Seaside Heights.

Pamplona…
Existential yet
beyond existence,
pure essence, essential.

Marilyn Kiss

Pamplona,
in July.

Sacrament

Peeling

The eyelid off the eye
The skin off the grape
The crust off the host

The senses

Open for ablution.

There is communion.

The host.
The body of the brute
The blood
The sacrifice of the runners

It is religious

It is holy

It is ungodly.

Marilyn Kiss
Pacharán Doubts

What if I don't write the oneiric?
What if I can't convey the fervor?
What if my words fail to evoke
the pacharán essence of festival dreams?

What if I fail
to maintain the fresh splendor
of virgin snow on January 1
as the song resurges?

What if my scribblings
cannot feed the February hunger?

What if March comes and goes
and there is no relief in my poems?

April arrives, coquettishly,
and my verses wander through
the quotidian streets of Pamplona.

On the fifth of May,
my pen oozes with adulation,
longing, desire for San Fermín.

By June, my doubts overcome me.
Pacharán awaits me.
The pen needs ink.

It is July.
Confidence returns.
There are pacharán days,
pacharán nights,
pacharán dreams.

The bulls are running in Pamplona.

A Pamplona Poem

> *Scatter my ashes...*
> —À la Miguel Piñero

Many more times before I die
I want to visualize
Pacharán dreams
I want to experience
the Fiesta,
I want to honor San Fermín---

then scatter my ashes
along the well-traveled routes
of my beloved journey

From Bar Txoko
to the Cervecería Tropicana
from Heladería Gofrera Jon
to La Caixa
from Foto Auma
to Hotel La Perla
from Casino Eslava to
Bar Sevilla and the Windsor
from Iruña Bar
to the ATH at the
Banco Bilbao Vizcaya,
scatter handfuls of my ashes.

"There is no other place for me to be"
since the sites of deepest living
deserve the ashes of final becoming,
the existential transformation
into one's own self

A rebellious daughter
I have been,
stealing away to Spain,
my home away from home.

Marilyn Kiss

An avid reveler
I have been,
enjoying the elusive moment,
not planning for the future.

A complex adult
I have been,
sneaking into depression,
my escape from escaping.

A pretender I have been,
inauthentic,
a false poet
an untrained photographer
an unfulfilled professor
but a staunch teacher,
a believer in the decisive moment,
in the emotion expressed.

A true traveler and lover,
I have been,
though sparingly acquainted
with the deep meanings of
friendship.

"So here I am, look at me"
proud to write about
Pamplona
to share its
Pacharán dreams
to invite you to
Hemingway's rising sun.

I don't want
to be buried in Missouri
I don't want
to rest in a Staten Island cemetery
I don't want to be
in a box

Pacharán Dreams

I want to feel the pounding hooves,
the midnight dancers,
the dawn revelers,
I want them to saturate my remains
with spilled Pacharán.

So please, *por favor,* when I die
take my ashes to Pamplona
and scatter them along the Estafeta.

Then share a bottle
of Zoco
and dream,
dream,
dream.

About the Author

Marilyn Kiss is Associate Professor of Spanish at Wagner College, Staten Island, New York. She was director of Study Abroad for 17 years and believes strongly in international education since her first experiences studying in Mexico and Spain were transformative in her own life and deepened her love for things Hispanic. She and her companion, Miguel Angel, are avid photographers, cinephiles, peace activists and vegetarians. They hope to experience many more *Sanfermines* in Pamplona… without eating any *estofado de toro*.

Photo by miguelÁngel

www.ingramcontent.com/pod-product-compliance
Lightning Source LLC
Chambersburg PA
CBHW052110070526
44584CB00017B/2422